RAIN FOREST
BIRDS

Text and Photography by Edward Parker

RAINTREE
STECK-VAUGHN
PUBLISHERS

A Harcourt Company

Austin   New York
www.raintreesteckvaughn.com

Copyright Permissions, Steck-Vaughn Company,
P.O. Box 26015, Austin, TX 78755.

Published by Raintree Steck-Vaughn Publishers,
an imprint of Steck-Vaughn Company

Library of Congress Cataloging-in-Publication Data is available upon request.

ISBN 0-7398-5239-6

Printed in Hong Kong. Bound in the United States.

1 2 3 4 5 6 7 8 9 0 LB 07 06 05 04 03 02

Editor: Sarah Doughty
Design: Bernard Higton
Text consultant: Dr Paul Toyne

Picture acknowledgments:
All photographs are by Edward Parker with the exception of the following:
OSF 7 (John Chellman), 9 top (Robin Bush), 13 left (Kjell Sandved), 15 (Konrad Wothe), 18 bottom (Michael Sewell), 21 top (Tui de Roy), 25 (Joe B. Blossom), 27 and cover (Michael Fogden), 33 top (Eric Woods), 45 top (Michael Fogden).

CONTENTS

1 WELCOME TO THE RAIN FOREST

◄ *This brightly colored taveta golden weaver bird is typical of many small birds that live in the rain forest along coastal areas of East Africa.*

The Rain Forest Home

Birds live in all regions of the earth, from the coldest places at the North and South Poles to the heat of the tropics. The rain forests lie around the equator between the tropics of Cancer and Capricorn, where temperatures are high throughout the year and the annual rainfall is greater than 79 inches (2,000 mm). Tropical rain forests are found in parts of South and Central America, Africa, Southeast Asia, and Australia. They are home to some of the world's most beautiful birds.

In the rain forests, there are more species of birds than in any other habitat on Earth. In the Amazon rain forest of South America, toucans and macaws fly high in the canopy while tiny hummingbirds dart from flower to flower. In the African rain forests, the screams of huge hornbills can be heard as they glide over the tallest trees. In Australia, giant flightless birds called cassowaries race headfirst through the vegetation on the forest floor. In Southeast Asia, brilliantly colored birds of paradise put on remarkable displays to their mates to show off their plumage.

Fascinating Fact

When a hummingbird hovers in front of a flower, it beats its wings so fast that it makes a humming sound.

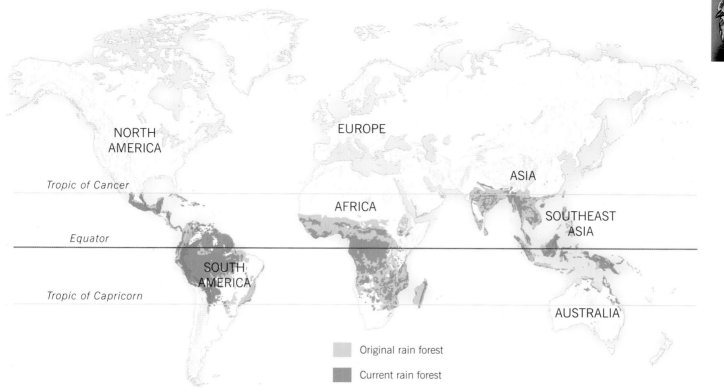

NORTH
AMERICA

Tropic of Cancer

Equator

SOUTH
AMERICA

Tropic of Capricorn

EUROPE

ASIA

AFRICA

SOUTHEAST
ASIA

AUSTRALIA

Original rain forest

Current rain forest

Source: *World Conservation Monitoring Center*

▲ A map showing the extent of the world's tropical rain forests today, compared with their coverage 500 years ago, before large-scale deforestation began.

▼ Several species of macaw live in the Amazon rain forest. The scarlet macaw is one of the most brilliantly colored birds of the Amazon.

The Variety of the Rain Forest

Rain forest birds share their rain forest home with many species of mammals, insects, spiders, reptiles, and amphibians. They thrive on the plentiful plants and insects of the tropical rain forests. Of all the rain forest animals, birds are the most easily observed as they fly between the trees. This book will focus on the variety of birds in the Amazon rain forest.

The lowland forest of the Amazon is home to a wide variety of birds, from eagles to parrots.

Types of Rain Forest

Rain forests are divided into two main types, according to their height above sea level. These are lowland forest and tropical montane forest. Lowland forests are the most widespread stretches of rain forest. They contain the majority of bird species, from parrots to giant monkey-eating eagles. Tropical montane forests occur on hills and mountains above 3,000 feet (900 m), where conditions are generally cooler. The trees in these rain forests are typically shorter than in lowland forests and are often hidden in dense mists, giving rise to their alternative name, "cloud forests." The dense tangled vegetation of tropical montane forests is home to many unique species of birds such as pygmy owls and trogons. In South America, it is mainly in the tropical montane forests that the unique hummingbird is found.

Tropical montane forest is cooler than lowland forest and has different vegetation. Tropical montane forest is home to some unique species of birds.

The Importance of Birds

Birds are a vital part of the rain forest ecology and an important part of the food web. Predators such as eagles feed on small mammals, while flycatchers, which are perching birds, feed on insects.

RAIN FOREST SECRETS

BIRDS OF PARADISE

There are 42 species of birds that are known as birds of paradise, and they are some of the most colorful birds in the rain forest.

Birds of paradise are found mainly in lowland forest in Papua New Guinea in South-east Asia. The group includes many birds with decorative feathers. The males show their colourful plumes when they dance to attract the females.

The male king bird of paradise (see right), which, like most birds of paradise, lives in the tropical montane forest of Papua New Guinea in Southeast Asia, is typical of the species. The male bird is brightly colored and has two wire-like tail feathers with a swirl of green barbs (decorative tufts) that are used in his courtship display as he swings upside down, calling to the females. The females choose their mates after watching the displays of the males.

Fascinating Fact

Parrots can easily grip fruits and nuts because their feet have opposing claws—two of their toes face forward and two face backward.

Birds also provide food for other rain forest animals. Many mammals, such as jaguars and monkeys, are predators and feed on birds and their eggs. Even some of the larger insects and spiders occasionally include small birds as part of their diet.

Many birds have lifestyles that are important for the survival of species of plants. Some birds, such as parrots and hummingbirds, help to pollinate rain forest flowers. Fruit-eating birds are also important in dispersing seeds. Toucans, parrots, and quetzals eat fruit and carry the seeds, which they cannot digest, in their stomachs for many miles before expelling them.

② THE DIVERSITY OF BIRDS

Some types of birds, such as gulls, are common throughout the world, and different species can be found both in temperate and tropical climates.

The Range of Birds

There are many types of birds, such as herons, gulls, and vultures, that are able to live in a wide variety of habitats around the world, including rain forests. However, many species of rain forest birds have evolved to such specialized lifestyles that they can be found only in very small areas of particular rain forests. Hummingbirds, for example, have bills that are adapted to gaining nectar only from certain species of flowering rain forest plants.

Because of their ability to fly, birds have frequently colonized isolated rain forest islands. Over thousands of years, new species have evolved, as birds adapted to their new surroundings. Where there were no predators, many island species evolved into flightless birds, such as the dodo and the cassowary bird, for example.

The Papuan lorikeet is a colorful bird that lives on the island of Papua New Guinea.

The Variety of Birds

The world's rain forests contain many of the estimated 8,600 species of birds that live on the earth today. The color of rain forest birds ranges from the dull browns of the nightjar to the brilliant

RAIN FOREST SECRETS

THE CASSOWARY BIRD

The cassowary (see right) is a very large flightless bird that lives in the rain forests of Australia, Papua New Guinea, and Indonesia. It feeds mainly on fruits, berries, and seeds from the forest floor.

Over millions of years, cassowaries have evolved to become flightless birds. Unlike almost all other birds, their wings are quite small and their bones are heavy. Cassowaries are well adapted to life on the ground. They have huge, muscular legs for fast running and sharp-toed feet for defense. A cassowary has a bald but brightly colored head with a large horny ridge, which it holds forward to break the foliage ahead of it as it runs.

reds, greens, and blues of hummingbirds and parrots. The wide variety of species and huge range of colors mask the fact that birds are the least varied of all groups of animals.

To enable them to fly, birds have remained fairly small and light compared with other animals. They have kept a similar basic shape, and their body structure is less varied than that of other groups, such as mammals.

◀ Like the hummingbird, the bill of the pygmy honeyeater from Papua New Guinea is specially adapted for feeding on nectar.

A Bird's Body

In many ways, birds are similar to mammals. Like mammals, birds are descended from reptiles, and they are also warm-blooded. Birds also have four limbs like mammals, but these are made up of two legs and two wings. Sight and hearing are a bird's two main senses, and, like humans, a bird has a poor sense of smell. The main difference between mammals and birds is the way that birds have evolved for flight. Birds have developed huge flight muscles and a unique system of respiration. While mammals have lungs for breathing, birds use air sacs as well as lungs. This greatly improves the flow of oxygen to their heart and wing muscles.

The Skeleton

Over millions of years, birds have gradually developed lightweight bones to help reduce their weight. Many of a bird's major bones such as its leg bones are hollow. Others have been greatly decreased in size to save weight.

▲ An anaco parrot showing its features—feathers, wings, claws, and a lightweight bill.

◀ The masked flower-piercer from the tropical montane forest of Ecuador. This bird has a bill designed to puncture the base of flowers, which enables it to feed on the nectar.

REPTILIAN BIRDS

The earliest fossil ever found of a birdlike creature is called the archaeopteryx. "Archaeo" refers to ancient rocks and "pteryx" means "wing." The "fossil bird" was found in rocks in a quarry in Germany. The rocks date from the Jurassic period, around 160 million years ago.

This replica of the original fossil (see right) shows an animal that was halfway between a reptile and a bird. The head, jaw, and tail were like those of a reptile, but it also had wings and feathers and could possibly fly. Because it had claws on its wings, many scientists believe that it probably clambered around in the trees and glided between them using its feather-covered wings and tail. It is believed that the bird's feathers developed from special reptile scales and evolved to help the bird keep warm.

◀ The hollow leg bones of large birds like herons help to reduce their weight, making flying easier.

Evolution has reduced the skull in size and weight to produce a lightweight head. Lightweight bills have replaced the heavy jawbones and teeth found in other animals. A bird's forelimbs, which are like the bones in the arms and fingers of humans, have been transformed into wings. Birds have evolved a very specialized breastbone, which not only is light but has a large surface area for the attachment of the bird's powerful wing muscles.

Lungs and Heart

The process of taking off, especially for large birds like herons and flamingos, requires huge amounts of energy. The respiratory system of a bird allows it to breathe very efficiently. The bird's air sacs help to speed up the rate at which air enters the lungs. This system enables the bird to provide the necessary oxygen required by the heart and wing muscles during the stress of taking off. To assist, the heart is also capable of beating much faster than a mammal's heart and helps the blood to pump quickly around the body. The hearts of small tropical finches can reach rates of over 500 beats per minute, while the hearts of hummingbirds can reach over 1,250 beats per minute.

▼ *Flamingos in Mexico's mangrove forest. These large birds require a huge amount of energy and plenty of oxygen to help them take off from the ground or from the water.*

THE FEATHERS OF THE ARGUS PHEASANT

Argus pheasants live in the rain forests of Malaysia and have the largest feathers of any bird. Like the peacock, the argus pheasant has a magnificent tail display. The male attracts a female to a rain forest "dancefloor" on a hill to show off its feathers. Toward the climax of the male's courtship dance, the argus pheasant reveals his plumage in all its glory. He throws up his wing feathers, revealing the previously hidden "eyes" on his broad secondary feathers. The result is an almost three-dimensional impression of hundreds of "eyes" looking at the chosen female.

Wings and Feathers

Feathers are one of the main features of birds, and they are strong and light. Each feather is made of a hollow central shaft, with lots of slender branches called barbs. The feathers on the back edge of the wing and the tail are the bird's longest feathers.

▲ *The secondary feathers on the head of this hummingbird are a beautiful shade of metallic green.*

They are called the primary feathers and they enable it to fly. The wings of small birds such as finches and thrushes are ideal for short flights between trees. Long wings, such as those of the frigate bird, are designed for long-distance flights. Secondary feathers cover the whole body and provide a smooth surface, which helps reduce wind resistance. Air is also trapped beneath a bird's feathers, forming a layer of insulation. Feathers of soft down grow under the secondary layer and help to keep the bird warm.

Bills

Birds of different species have evolved a wide range of bills. Each bill is specially designed for a particular method of feeding. Each species of hummingbird, for example, has a bill that fits the shape of particular flowers it feeds on. Parrots have hugely powerful bills, which they use to crack nuts and tear unripe fruit. Some birds, such as water hawks, have strong, hooked bills that they use for tearing meat.

▶ *These brown pelicans use their huge bills to catch fish when they dive into the water.*

RAIN FOREST SECRETS

TOUCAN BILLS

Toucans, which live in Central and South America, can have bills that grow longer than the rest of their bodies. Their bills are hard and sharp, but they are also thin and light.

For toucans the color of the bill is more important than the color of the plumage, because their bill helps to frighten away possible predators.

In the Amazon rain forest, there are two species of toucan that like to eat food from the same trees. The stronger species defends the best fruit trees against competition from other birds. The weaker species, however, imitates the coloring of the bill and plumage of the larger one. Although it is a smaller bird, this makes it possible for it to feed in the trees of the stronger species. The weaker bird has to remain quiet so as not to give itself away with its different call.

▼ *When eating, a parrot uses its feet to hold the fruit and its strong beak to tear the flesh away from the inner kernel.*

Herons have long bills for catching fish in shallow water. The flamingo has a strange bill designed to sift small shellfish out of the mud at the bottom of lagoons. Some species of pelican have huge bills, over 20 inches (500 mm) in length, which they use like a net to catch fish.

Digestion

The way birds eat and digest food, without the need for heavy jaws or teeth, has evolved to keep their bodies light for flying. Birds have a chamber in their throat that is rather like a pouch. This is called a crop, or the first stomach. Food can be stored in the crop and also crushed down into smaller pieces. After being in the crop, the food is passed to the gizzard, which is the second stomach. Once the food is inside the gizzard, the muscles grind it up with the help of grit (sand or gravel) swallowed by the bird.

This black-fronted nunbird from South America lives deep in the rain forest. It finds a perch among the lower branches of the trees and watches for insects, which it catches in midair.

Types of Lowland Forest

Rain forests that are found in different parts of the world often look similar, but have unique conditions and species of birds that are not found anywhere else. The most widespread type of rain forest is lowland forest, which exists in the Amazon basin. Here, the main division is between *terra firme* (dry ground) forest and *várzea* (flooded forest). The main feature of flooded forests is that they remain underwater for several months of each year. Another important type of lowland forest is mangrove forest, which is a specialized type of rain forest that lines about one-fourth of all tropical coastlines.

▼ This smooth-billed ani from the lowland forest of the Amazon is not a strong flyer, so it feeds mainly on insects and fallen fruit on the forest floor.

RAIN FOREST SECRETS

GUANS

Guans, such as the crested guan (see below), live in the drier parts of the lowland forest, from Mexico down to Brazil. Guans are mainly tree-dwelling birds. They can be seen moving in small groups across the treetops, although they will come to the ground to gorge on fallen fruit and to drink water. Guans can be easily heard because they have a loud, booming call that carries a long distance through the rain forest.

Male and female guans are very similar in appearance. During mating season, the males perform a wing-drumming display, making a whirring sound to attract a mate. Once they are paired as breeding partners, guans usually make a bulky nest in the tallest tree they can find, to rear their young.

▲ *Many species of parrot live in the* terra firme *forest of the Amazon, feeding on fruits and nuts.*

Dry Ground Forest

In the Amazon rain forest, around 80 percent of the total area is *terra firme* forest. Crested guans, many types of parrot, and toucans are just a few of the species living in *terra firme* forest. *Terra firme* forest also has species of trees and other plants that are not found in other types of rain forest. Some species of birds, such as the tyrian metaltail hummingbird and the hyacinth macaw, are specially adapted to feed on these trees and plants. Other bird species, such as the crested guan or the currasow, survive on very specific types of fruits, seeds, and leaves found only in the *terra firme* forest.

▲ The changing water level of the flooded forest provides ideal conditions for birds that feed on fish, such as herons and egrets.

Flooded Forest

Flooded forests occur in rain forests all around the world, but the largest and most famous example is the flooded forest in the upper Amazon, near the city of Manaus in Brazil. Here the water levels fall and rise between the dry and wet seasons, so the area is completely flooded in the wet season. The types of trees that can survive this flooding are very different from those that are found in the *terra firme* forests. The flooded forest provides a wide range of habitats, from large trees where birds such as hoatzins feed, to

RAIN FOREST SECRETS

THE HOATZIN

Hoatzins (see below right) are unusual birds that have evolved uniquely in the flooded forest of the Amazon river basin. Because there is little dry land, the young hoatzins have three hooks where their wings bend, to help them remain in the trees. These hooks act like claws when they are moving through the rain forest branches. Young hoatzins also have claws on their first and second toes, which they use to grasp the trees. This helps them to move like tree-living lizards through the flooded forest.

Hoatzins feed on waterside vegetation. They eat the new leaves, flowers, and fruits of trees such as cecropia and black mangrove. Their digestive system is specially

adapted to process leaves that other animals cannot digest. A hoatzin's crop is fifty times larger than its second stomach, where its diet of tough leaves is further digested.

shallow wetlands where a variety of herons and ibises catch food. The larger waterways are ideal for anhingas (snakebirds) and kingfishers.

Mangrove Forest

Mangrove forest grows in mud at the edges of seas and rivers. Mangrove forest is made up of trees with "breathing" roots, to overcome the wet, salty conditions. These roots stick out above the water line and allow the trees to take in oxygen from the air. Mangrove forests are home to many species of birds and are particularly important for nesting seabirds and migrating flocks. Plenty of fish lay their eggs here, so many fish-eating birds live in the mangrove forests. Birds such as the mangrove hummingbird, the frigate bird, and many species of wading bird live in this type of habitat.

▲ The anu from Brazil spends much of its time close to the edge of rivers and among mangrove roots.

Tropical Montane Forest

There are many species of birds that live in tropical montane forest. It is home to various species of trogon, owl, vulture, hummingbird, and ant pita. The trees are covered in many types of plants called epiphytes, including orchids and bromeliads. Birds such as hummingbirds feed on the nectar of these rain forest flowers. Many of the species of hummingbird that live in these habitats are very rare because so little untouched tropical montane forest remains.

◄ The rufus-naped brush finch is found only in the tropical montane forests of Ecuador and Colombia.

Herons are a group of birds that have adapted to live near water in many parts of the world. This heron is flying to a different feeding ground in the flooded forest of the Amazon.

Divisions by Lifestyle

Birds are often divided into groups that have similar lifestyles or distinctive features. Birds of prey, parrots, gamebirds, pigeons, and hummingbirds are just a few examples of the major groups of birds that live in the rain forests. Species of many of these groups are also found in other parts of the world. For example, it is possible to see different species of gulls in the Amazon rain forest, northern Europe, and North America. Herons, storks, and kingfishers are other types of birds whose different species can be found both in the tropical rain forest and in temperate parts of the world. The lifestyles of the main groups of rain forest birds are explained in this chapter.

Vultures are commonly seen within the rain forests, but are also found scavenging in towns and villages.

Birds of Prey

Birds of prey include vultures, eagles, kites, buzzards, falcons, and fish eagles, such as the endangered African fish eagle from West Africa. Some of the world's largest species of birds, such as the king vulture, are birds of prey.

THE HARPY EAGLE

The harpy eagle is the world's largest eagle and is found in areas of untouched rain forest throughout Central and South America. This harpy eagle chick (see right) is from the Amazon rain forest in Peru. Each of its feet will grow to the size of a man's hand, and its lethally sharp talons will be used to grab its prey. The fully grown harpy eagle usually hits its prey at high speed, often killing it outright with the impact.

The harpy eagle mainly feeds on monkeys, sloths, coatimundis, opossums, and tree porcupines. It has unusually short wings for a bird of its size, allowing it to fly more easily between the dense rain forest trees.

▼ Despite their small size, scops owls are excellent hunters, preying on nocturnal mammals in the rain forests of Madagascar.

All birds, from the giant vulture to the tiny pygmy African falcon, share a number of specialized features. These include powerful legs, feet with sharp claws, superb eyesight, and a hooked bill. Many rain forest eagles, hawks, and owls are formidable hunters, while vultures are expert in scavenging the prey of other animals. Most birds of prey, such as the monkey-eating eagle, kill their victim with their claws. They can strike a sloth or monkey at great speed, often killing it immediately. A few species of eagle, however, kill their prey outright by a blow directly from their sharp, hooked bill.

Fascinating Fact

The crowned eagle can snatch monkeys from trees and small antelopes from the forest floor.

The Parrot Family

There are 330 species of parrot worldwide. They can be divided into three families: parrots, lorikeets (lories), and cockatoos, although cockatoos are not usually found in the rain forest.

Parrots

This family of parrots includes macaws, parrots, and parakeets (small parrots). The parrot family is found mainly in the rain forests of Australia, South America, and Southeast Asia. It includes many brilliantly colored birds that squawk and chatter loudly as they fly above the rain forest. They nest in tree hollows and feed largely on fruit, seeds, nectar, and fungi. They have highly specialized bills that they use for cracking nuts and tearing open fruit. Their bill can also be used as a "third foot," for holding on when climbing among a tree's branches.

The chestnut-fronted parrot, sometimes called the severe parrot, is found throughout the rain forests of the Americas, from Panama to Bolivia.

MACAWS

The macaw is a brightly colored bird found only in South America. It is the largest type of parrot and can measure over 3 feet (1 m) from its head to the tip of its tail. In the wild, macaws are among the noisiest of all birds, with their constant chatter of loud and tuneless squawks, shrieks, and clicks. Macaws are intelligent and playful and can be taught to mimic.

The scarlet macaw (see above) is one of the largest and most striking types of macaw. Scarlet macaws form breeding pairs for life, which can be longer than 30 years. Like most parrots they feed on fruits, nuts, and berries, and nest in the hollows of trees.

▶ *All types of parrot, such as these hyacinth macaws, tend to group together and nest in the hollows of large trees.*

▼ *The black-capped lorikeet lives on the island of Papua New Guinea.*

Many parakeets are fast fliers, and South American macaws are excellent fliers even though they are larger than parakeets. While the macaws are usually multicolored, most parrots tend to be mainly green.

Lorikeets

The lorikeets form a distinct subgroup within the parrot family. There are over fifty species of lorikeet, most of which occur throughout the rain forests of Indonesia, Papua New Guinea, Australia, and the islands of the Pacific. Lorikeets are treetop birds and tend to fly in large, noisy groups between flowering trees. Like macaws, they are brightly colored and they are generally smaller than most parrots. However, the feature that sets them apart from the other types of parrot is their brushlike tongue, which they use to extract nectar and pollen from rain forest flowers.

Lorikeets are well known for their theatrical displays as well as for their stunning plumage. The rainbow lorikeet, for example, has up to thirty special gestures such as hopping, walking, and preening, which it exhibits in its dances. These displays are used to frighten off other males and attract females to mate.

Gamebirds

There are 263 species of gamebird worldwide. This group includes pheasants and currasows. In the rain forests of Africa and Southeast Asia, these birds live mainly on the ground, where they can find plenty of food. In South and Central America, they prefer to live in the trees because there is more food in the trees than on the forest floor. Gamebirds, with their rounded bodies, are hunted for food by rain forest people. In other parts of the world, gamebirds are domesticated. These species of birds are closely related to the rain forest varieties.

Pheasants

There are over 150 species of pheasant worldwide. Pheasants can be divided into three main groups: partridges, quails, and true pheasants. Pheasants usually have plump, rounded bodies, powerful wings, and long, unfeathered legs. Most pheasants can fly only short distances and live on the ground, digging for seeds to eat. Most species are found in

▲ Gamebirds have a similar basic shape, with a rounded body, strong wings, and long legs. This is the female roulroul partridge of Southeast Asia.

◄ It is fairly common among species of pheasant for the male to be quite different in color from the female. This male roulroul is also clearly identified by his red brushlike crest.

RAIN FOREST SECRETS

RED JUNGLE FOWL

One rain forest bird that is familiar to millions of people who do not live near the rain forest is the red jungle fowl (see right). This is the ancestor of the domestic chicken and originally inhabited many parts of Southeast Asia. Like many other types of pheasant, the male red jungle fowl has striking plumage. It displays feathers in a wide range of colors such as iridescent green, gold, and chestnut and has a brilliant red, fleshy comb on its head. The less colorful females are varying shades of brown and chestnut.

Like other pheasants from Africa and Southeast Asia, the red jungle fowl is a ground-living bird, usually seen in large groups. Flocks of jungle fowl spend much of their time digging on the forest floor looking for insects, seeds, fallen fruit, and young shoots.

Southeast Asia, but a few species are found in Africa. The types of pheasant that are found in these different parts of the world include the Congo peacock, the red jungle fowl of Sumatra and Java, the argus pheasant of Malaysia, and the roulroul partridge of Sumatra and Borneo.

Currasows

Currasows are a group of 44 species of gamebird (including guans) that live in the rain forests of South and Central America. Although they live mainly in the trees and will only occasionally visit the forest floor to collect fallen fruit, currasows are large birds that appear clumsy when moving about in the high branches. The great currasow is typical of this group of birds. Like guans, currasows are well known for their booming calls. The calls of the nocturnal currasow can be heard echoing through the rain forest at night. There is one currasow known as a chacalaca because of its unusual three-syllable call.

THE BLUE CROWNED PIGEON

Pigeons

There are over 300 species of pigeon (including doves) in this family, many of which are rain forest species. One of the most famous species of pigeon was the dodo, a giant flightless bird that lived on the island of Mauritius over 300 years ago. Dodos died out when they became a target for the visiting Dutch sailors looking for an easy meal. Also, rats and dogs from the sailors' ships ate the dodos' eggs or killed their chicks. Because of this, dodos eventually became extinct by 1681.

Today, most types of rain forest pigeon are found in Australia and Southeast Asia and can vary greatly in size. Species include the bleeding heart dove and the Victoria crested pigeon. Both male and female pigeons are unique because they secrete a milky substance from the lining of their crop to feed their young for the first few days.

▼ *A dove finds food, such as seeds and fruit, on the forest floor.*

The blue crowned pigeon is native to the rain forests of northwest Papua New Guinea, where it lives in muddy lowland forest. The blue-crowned pigeon is among the largest of the pigeon groups. On its head it has a beautiful, distinctive crest of fan-shaped, lacy feathers.

Like all members of the pigeon family, the males and females are similar in appearance but display very different courtship behavior. Pigeons live together in small groups and form mating pairs for life, which is unusual for ground-living birds. Both parents take their turn in sitting on the two eggs that are laid, until they hatch 28 days later.

▲ *A hummingbird hovering at nectar-producing flowers to feed. Hummingbirds also catch mosquitoes and other small insects as part of their diet.*

Fascinating Fact

Hummingbirds have special wing muscles that allow them to flap their wings at up to 80 beats per second.

Hummingbirds

There are 320 species of hummingbird in South America. Because of their size and body structure, they form a unique group. Most species are very small; the frilled coquette from Brazil, for example, weighs less than .11 ounces (3g). Many species of hummingbird are well adapted to living in the rain forest. At 5 inches (120 mm) in length, the sword-billed hummingbird has the longest bill of any bird in relation to its body. This allows it to probe the nectar deep in the trumpet-shaped flowers it feeds on in the tropical montane forest of Venezuela. Hummingbirds are exceptional fliers. They are able to fly forward, sideways, and backward, as well as hover and even fly upside down.

Rain Forest Waterbirds and Wading Birds

Many rain forest bird species are adapted to living beside waterways and lakes. These groups of birds include herons, ducks, kingfishers, darters, cormorants, storks, and many other types of waders and gulls. In the Amazon rain forest, waterbirds and wading birds take advantage of the great changes in the level of the water between the seasons. Large flocks of birds can be seen around small lakes, where fish become trapped in the dry season.

Herons

There are over sixty species of heron worldwide. Rain forest herons are medium- to large-sized birds. They have long necks and legs, slim bodies, and broad wings. Herons hunt in varying depths of water. They can wade or remain motionless, catching fish and other creatures in their dagger-shaped bills. Herons have special down feathers on their chests, which produce a powder. After feeding, this powder is used to clean the greasy marks left on their chests from catching and eating fish.

◀ *(Above left) An Amazonian moorhen is a waterbird that is common along the waterways of the Amazon rain forest.*

▲ *(Above right) Herons are wading birds that move slowly through the shallow waters, waiting to snatch small fish with their long bills.*

RAIN FOREST SECRETS

THE JACANA WATERBIRD

This family of waterbirds is easy to identify because all the birds have large feet in relation to their bodies. Jacanas have evolved very long toes and claws, which help them distribute their weight over wide areas. This helps jacanas to move over floating plants such as lilies, and has given rise to their alternative name, "lily-trotters."

In the Amazon rain forest, jacanas usually feed on small fish, insects, and seeds of aquatic plants. Although they are poor fliers, they are excellent at swimming and diving.

The jacanas are well camouflaged by their color as they move among the floating vegetation.

◀ *These Amazonian pato da cristas are found in large flocks on lakes and slow-moving rivers throughout the Amazon rain forest.*

Ducks

There are more than 140 species of duck worldwide, many of which live in the rain forests. The wet conditions are ideal for ducks that obtain plant and animal food from either the surface of the water or the bottom of a lake or river. Rain forest species include the large muscovy duck and the pato da crista, which can often be seen in large flocks in the Amazon.

Cormorants

There are around thirty species of cormorants worldwide and they are found in many different habitats, including the rain forests. The reed cormorant, for example, lives in West Africa and Madagascar. Like other cormorants it is a fairly large, web-footed bird with a strongly hooked bill. A shag is another name for a cormorant.

Darters

There are four species of darter, all of which are tropical varieties, found in South and Central America. Both cormorants and darters specialize in catching fish. They dive into the water with their wings held to their sides in order to catch their prey. From the surface they sometimes dive deep underwater, paddling downward using their webbed feet. Cormorants and darters are commonly seen drying off on perches at the edge of rivers and lakes.

▲ *The long-tailed shag is a member of the cormorant family and lives along the rain forest rivers of Cameroon and Nigeria in Africa.*

RAIN FOREST SECRETS

THE AMAZONIAN SNAKEBIRD

The anhinga is a type of darter that lives along the edges of rivers throughout the Amazon rain forest. Locally, it is called a snakebird because when it is swimming, only its head and long neck can be seen above the water. From its swimming position, it usually dives over 16 feet (5 m) underwater. Darters have evolved a body that is not designed to float well, so it can dive more effectively.

When the snakebird has finished diving for food, it comes to the surface to dry off. Like other types of cormorants or darters, snakebirds are a common sight on perches at the edge of rivers and lakes, where they sit with their wings spread out, drying in the sun.

▼ *Kingfishers like to find a perch above a river, where they dive to catch small fish and insects.*

Kingfishers

There are 86 species of kingfisher worldwide. Most of these are tropical varieties and are brightly colored. Kingfishers have a distinctive bill that is always straight, with a pointed tip. Many kingfishers catch fish and insects by diving from a perch above the water. However, most species of kingfisher feed on dry land, catching snakes, insects, and lizards. They usually nest in burrows along the banks of rivers.

6 DISAPPEARING BIRDS

Like this bird, many species of bird of paradise are in danger of becoming extinct in the wild because of the effects of deforestation.

Fascinating Fact

Due to tropical deforestation, about 100 species of birds a day become extinct.

Many species of rain forest birds have been pushed to the brink of extinction over the last hundred years. It is likely that many of the rarest birds will no longer exist in the wild before the end of the 21st century. The glaucous macaw from South America has already become extinct. There are many reasons for the decline in rain forest species, but they are mainly caused by the activities of humans. These include habitat destruction, introducing new forms of agriculture, pollution, hunting birds for food, collecting birds for the pet trade, and indirectly killing birds by introducing predators.

An area of tropical montane forest that has been cut down and is beginning to regenerate. The renewed rain forest will not support the same variety of bird species as the original rain forest.

Habitat Destruction

It is estimated that one million acres (400,000 hectares) of rain forest in the Amazon are being cut down each year to produce timber, firewood, charcoal, and wood pulp for paper. Vast areas are also being converted into agricultural land. Soybean production in the Amazon rain forest, African oil palm plantations in West Africa, and

Hornbills

There are many different species of hornbill in the rain forests of Africa and Southeast Asia. They include the helmeted hornbill and wreathed hornbill (see right) of Southeast Asia and the pied hornbill of West Africa. Many species of hornbill have a distinctive long bill with an extension that resembles a horn.

Several species of hornbill are severely affected by logging. Hornbills make their nests in mature trees, but these trees may be burned when the best timber from the rain forest is removed.

Research in West Africa has shown that as soon as a new logging road is cut through an area of primary rain forest in countries like Sierra Leone, species such as the pied hornbill retreat into another patch of untouched forest. This means that large parts of the African rain forest no longer contain hornbills.

rice cultivation in Southeast Asia have caused the loss of millions of acres of rain forest. Building dams, digging mines, and expanding towns and cities have also led to

▼ *Making way for cattle ranches has had a severe effect on birds in South and Central America.*

rain forest loss. As rain forests are reduced to smaller and smaller fragments, not only do bird species disappear, but the migration routes of many birds also become disrupted.

Rain forest birds are harmed by changes to their habitat. The draining of wetlands to create new farmland means that waterfowl and wading birds no longer have homes. Logging removes many of the large trees where parrots and birds of prey breed. The burning of the fallen timber affects those species that feed on the insects and fungi that live in decaying logs.

Eggs, Feathers, and Skins

Many rain forest bird species are highly prized for their eggs, feathers, and even their skins. In the 18th and 19th centuries, for example, it was fashionable to wear shawls made of hummingbird skins. Egg collectors have also drastically reduced the wild populations of birds such as eagles and parrots. It takes a long time for these birds to become old enough to lay eggs, and when they are of breeding age they lay only a few eggs each year. Feathers have also been fashionable during recent years, and many species, including the bird of paradise, are still trapped for their valuable plumage and smuggled in huge numbers to the United States and Europe.

▲ Colorful feathers are collected from trapped birds as fashionable items.

The Pet Trade

The capture of rain forest birds for the pet trade has had a serious effect on the numbers of certain species. Parrots are just one example of birds that have been caught in the thousands to provide pets for people. Now there are fewer than 500 parrots of the St. Lucia species left in the Caribbean, because they have been captured for the pet trade. The African Gray parrot is also threatened. It is one of the most popular and talkative of parrots. It lives in large groups in the rain forests of West, Central, and East Africa. The birds roost together on tall trees along the edges of lakes and follow regular routes to and from their roosts each day. Their habits in the wild make the African Grays easy to catch.

▶ Parrots are popular pets throughout the world. This woman from Ecuador shows how tame her pet is.

RAIN FOREST SECRETS

CAGED BIRDS

The first record of a caged parrot occurred in Greece around 400 B.C. Ever since then parrots have been popular as pets, especially since they are able to mimic speech in various languages. Soon after Americans discovered tropical parrots living in South and Central America, they were exported to collectors in Europe.

This fascination for caged parrots has continued up until the present day. It has led to a huge reduction in the number of birds in the rain forests. The international trade in birds has lessened in the last 20 years, but in many developing countries it is part of the local culture to have a caged bird in the home.

In Brazil, Costa Rica, Thailand, Liberia, and in many other countries, rain forest birds are still being caught and sold in large numbers.

Hunting

Rain forest birds are hunted for a living and for sport. In many poor countries, bird meat provides protein for rural families. In Brazil, both toucans and ducks are hunted for food. In many cultures, shooting a bird of prey is a ritual part of growing up. Tourists also kill some birds for sport, while birds of prey are shot on sight by farmers who mistakenly think that all birds will attack their animals.

◄ *In remote areas, rain forest people hunt birds like this toucan to supplement their meager diets.*

Pollution and the production of vast quantities of trash from rain forest cities is affecting local bird populations. Some birds disappear, while scavengers like vultures often increase in number.

Pollution

Many birds are at the top of the food chain and feed on other creatures, such as insects. Because they are controlled by pesticides such as DDT, insects often have poisonous chemicals inside their bodies, which are then eaten by predatory birds. Such chemicals are known to affect the breeding of hawks and falcons, causing their eggshells to be thinner. They can also affect rain forest birds by killing insects, which are their main food. Pollution in the air, especially poisonous metals such as lead and cadmium from cars and pollution from industry, is also known to build up on the wing feathers of birds. This is taken into the body when a bird preens itself.

Agriculture

Converting areas of rain forest to plantations for agriculture can have serious effects on local bird populations. The setting up of large oil palm plantations in Cameroon, for example, has created "avian deserts," where only a few rain forest birds can continue to survive. Chemicals are often used to poison birds that try and feed on the crops. Burning the forest floor to prepare land for agriculture can kill off insects such as army ants, but these are vital foods to ant birds and other species of rain forest bird.

Millions of square miles of rain forest have been destroyed by fire, as people convert the rain forest into agricultural land. This kills off insects that are an important food for birds.

Agricultural Projects

Developing large-scale agricultural projects in rain forest areas has led to the numbers of birds declining rapidly. These create areas of "avian desert."

African oil palm plantations usually occupy land that was once teeming with a huge variety of bird species. Few birds feed on oil palm, and those that do are trapped or shot to ensure the best harvest for the farmers. In this way, many species of rain forest bird lose both their source of food and their home. Every few years, plantations are cleared of oil palms and they become deserted areas (see right), while the ground recovers.

Many birds that live deep inside the rain forest are affected by the service roads and other open spaces caused by the creation of plantations. This is because birds do not like to fly across open spaces between areas of forest. Eventually, groups of birds become isolated from others in small pockets of rain forest.

Introduction of Alien Species

Many species of rain forest bird are affected by the introduction of new predators. This has been particularly serious on rain forest islands where the introduction of domestic animals has led to the extinction of local birds. They are easily wiped out by the introduction of rats, pigs, and cats who prey on the birds, their young, or their eggs. Introducing other bird species may also be devastating for local birds. The parasitic shiny cowbird, for example, was introduced in the West Indies. This is a bird that pushes eggs out of other birds' nests, which has caused a serious decline in the local population of other birds.

By observing birds in the rain forests, scientists are trying to learn more about their behavior and habitat in order to help protect them.

Saving Birds

The wild populations of many rain forest birds such as the St. Lucia parrot and African fish eagle are critically low. Without help, these rain forest birds could become extinct within the next thirty years. Fortunately, there are many individuals and organizations that are working hard to help conserve the rain forests and the rare bird species that live in them. World Wildlife Federation (WWF), Birdlife International, the International Union of Bird Preservation (IUBP), and other organizations are all campaigning hard for the protection of rain forest habitats and endangered bird species.

Fascinating Fact

There are 47 threatened parrot species in South America and the Caribbean, and three in Africa and Madagascar.

A hummingbird is caught in a mist net. Researchers can weigh, measure, and tag the bird as part of their research, before releasing it.

Research

Research into bird numbers and the way birds live in the rain forest is a vital part of conservation. It is only by understanding the way that birds survive that proper conservation measures can be undertaken. Hummingbirds, for example, rely on only a few species of flowers for food.

▼ Conservation organizations are campaigning against large-scale projects because they cause so much damage to the habitats of rain forest birds.

Many species of parrot need a particular species of tree for their nesting sites. These trees must be allowed to mature enough to provide hollows to nest in. Many species of birds will not cross open areas such as those created by oil pipelines and roads. They need stretches of rain forest, or rain forest corridors, to link fragments of rain forest to each other.

LINKS

The Rio Mazan Project

In 1986, a water company in Ecuador, which owned an area of tropical montane forest close to the city of Cuenca, allowed a team of scientists to carry out a bird survey in the rain forest to identify the bird species present.

Like these researchers inspecting a hummingbird (see right), they recorded information about the birds before releasing each one. In the course of their survey, they observed some very rare species of birds including Andean toucans, ant pitas, trogons, and even Andean condors.

The results of the bird survey and the other research showed that although the area of rain forest was quite small, it had many species of birds that had disappeared from other parts of the Andes. When the surrounding habitat was destroyed, many birds had flown to this area of tropical montane forest, making it their home and producing a wide range of species in a small area. The outcome was the protection of the area for birds.

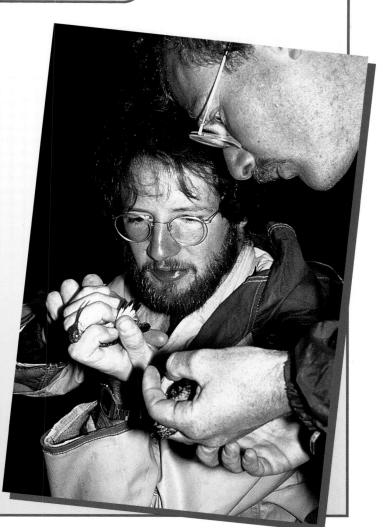

This group of children from Colombia are trying to help local bird species. They are replanting trees and creating rain forest corridors, linking patches of isolated rain forest.

Fascinating Fact

The Brazilian government has pledged to triple the area of protected rain forest in the Amazon to 100,000 sq. mi. (25 million hectares).

Some local people, such as this craftsman from Brazil, make souvenirs that appeal to people interested in rain forest birds.

Sharing the Rain Forest

For many indigenous peoples, such as the Yanomami of Brazil or the Baka pygmies of Cameroon, sharing the rain forest with animals and birds is part of their culture and their religious beliefs. However, most of the world's economy is based on exploiting resources as quickly and as cheaply as possible, with little thought for the future or the needs of the other living creatures that people share the world with.

Many conservation organizations, such as WWF, have been campaigning for governments, businesses, and individuals to use rain forest resources carefully, so as not to cause damage to the environment. Many logging companies have changed their practices. They now often only harvest the most valuable trees in the rain forest. The rest of the rain forest, which used to be felled and burned, is left standing for the benefit of the local wildlife and people.

The Hyacinth Macaw

The hyacinth macaw is one of the rarest parrots in Brazil, with a population of about 3,000 birds. It is one of the world's largest and most colorful parrots. Around half of these macaws live in the Amazon rain forest. The hyacinth macaw is a brilliant blue color and is easily seen as it flies between its favorite palm trees, searching for food. It is now so rare that tourists come from all over the world to see it in its natural habitat.

The hyacinth macaw is an ideal species to attract ecotourists to the Amazon rain forest.

Part of the money that comes from tourism can be used to help preserve the mature trees that the hyacinth macaw likes to nest in.

Ecotourism

Tourists will travel thousands of miles to see rare rain forest birds in their natural habitat. The industry that has developed, based around tourism, helps conservation in two ways. First, the governments of rain forest countries are reminded that their wildlife, including birds, attracts tourists and this has an economic value. Second, it shows that there are alternatives to damaging activities such as logging and cattle ranching. Ecotourism may encourage rain forest nations to slow down habitat destruction and help to protect the homes of rare bird species.

◀ *In some rain forest towns and cities, the value of the local wildlife is recognized and featured in unusual ways.*

Protected Areas

Some species of birds such as hornbills, harpy eagles, and parrots need large areas of rain forest in order to lead natural lives. Many rain forest birds also need to stop off in rain forest areas and wetlands when migrating to their breeding grounds. Organizations such as WWF have successfully campaigned for protected areas of rain forest to be set up all over the world. These can take the form of national parks, nature reserves, community-managed land, rain forest reserves, and certified rain forest areas. WWF has been campaigning for more rain forest corridors to link these protected areas.

International Law

Over the last few decades, many rare bird species have been given much more protection by introducing new international and national laws. In many countries, there are laws that aim to stop the hunting of rare birds for the pet trade and the collection of eggs.

▲ Birds that migrate long distances, such as pelicans, need areas of protected rain forest along the routes where they fly.

◀ The setting up of protected areas such as this area of rain forest in Australia will help to ensure the future for many types of rain forest birds.

Fascinating Fact

A new species of owl has recently been discovered in Ecuador in South America.

Lago Mamiraua

The ecological station called Lago Mamiraua in the Amazon rain forest is a vast area of flooded forest that is now protected and managed for the benefit of both the wildlife and the local population. It covers 2,777,000 acres (1,124,000 hectares) and is home to a variety of rare and endangered birds including the hoatzin, the very rare umbrella bird, and the great currasow.

Initially funded by WWF, the project at the ecological station has been so successful at improving the quality of life for the small rain forest communities and conserving the endangered wildlife that it is now used as a model in other parts of the Amazon rain forest.

▼ A weaver bird in the Korup National Rain Forest park, a protected area in Cameroon in West Africa.

There are also special international laws to prevent skins, feathers, bills, and other rare bird products from being traded around the world. The setting up of RAMSAR world heritage sites for the protection of important wetlands has given a number of rare migratory and wading birds a chance of survival.

Most countries around the world have signed the United Nations' International Convention on Biological Diversity. This is an agreement to help protect rare species from becoming extinct.

8 THE FUTURE

An Uncertain Future

The future of many rain forest birds is uncertain. Many species, such as the Spix's macaw, may be reduced to living in captivity in tiny numbers. It is likely that much rain forest will be destroyed in the next 30 years, and many species will no longer be able to survive in the wild.

Despite the efforts of environmental organizations and individuals, the only chance of long-term survival for many rain forest species lies in a change in attitude toward the way rain forests are used. However, more demands are being made on rain forest resources as the world's population increases. Most rain forests occur in the world's poorest countries, which often have little option but to exploit their natural resources to earn the money needed for development and repaying debt.

Assisting Birds

There are a number of ways the future of rain forest birds can be improved. These include reducing the numbers of birds caught for the pet trade, buying timber from

◀ *(Above left) This parrot species is being bred in captivity. Captive breeding helps to ensure that even if the species becomes extinct in the wild, a few birds will continue to exist.*

▲ *(Above right) Many species of macaw are endangered. Action now could help protect the unique habitats in which they live and could prevent many other species from becoming extinct.*

Fascinating Fact

In 1990, only one Spix's macaw remained in the wild in Brazil.

QUETZAL—GOD OF THE AIR

The quetzal is one of the most striking birds of Central and South America. It has a glittering emerald-green tail and wing feathers and a crimson front on its lower body. Its magnificent tail has two curving plumes that can reach over 3 feet (1 m) in length.

For ancient tribes of Central America such as the Aztecs, the quetzal was considered divine and it was worshiped as god of the air. Only the royal family was allowed to wear its tail feathers, which were removed from the live birds. Any common person who killed a quetzal was put to death.

The number of quetzals in the wild has dropped dramatically as the tropical montane forests have been cleared in its home range from southern Mexico to Panama, and because it has been hunted for souvenirs. The quetzal is the national bird of Mexico, and needs protection because of its rarity and its fascinating history.

plantations rather than from rain forests, and creating protected areas for rain forest birds to live in. The development of ecotourism, such as bird-watching vacations, is another way of protecting the birds' rain forest habitat while providing local people with a means of earning money.

Many economic activities that take place in the rain forests could be modified to have far less impact on the environment and the species that live in them. There are some less destructive economic choices than the large-scale logging, ranching, and agriculture practices that occur today. However, many of these activities are driven by the demands of the world's wealthiest countries. It is not only up to local people and governments, but also up to people and companies in the richer countries to alter their activities so that rain forest bird species and other rain forest wildlife can be offered a better future.

▶ *Understanding more about rain forest birds helps us find ways of protecting them.*

GLOSSARY

Jabiru stork.

air sacs Special thin-walled structures linked to the lungs that help improve respiration in birds.

alien An organism that is located in an area that is not its usual habitat.

bromeliads A group of plants that come from the Americas and have a rosette of spiny leaves.

camouflage Colors, shapes, and patterns that help any living thing blend in with its surroundings.

courtship display Special behavior, such as a dance or show of feathers, used by some species of birds to attract a mate.

crop A chamber or pouch, used by birds to store food in order to carry it back to the nest.

ecological station Under Brazilian law this is an area where both the traditional activities of the local people and the wildlife are protected.

ecotourism Encouraging people to visit an area because of its beauty and natural wildlife.

epiphytes Plants that grow on other plants.

evolved When a species of any organism has changed by natural processes over many generations.

extinct Died out. When the species of any organism no longer exists.

food web The totality of interacting food chains in an ecological community.

fossils The remains of organisms from millions of years ago, preserved in solid rock.

fungi A group of non-flowering plants, such as mushrooms or molds. They usually live on other plants.

habitat The natural home of living things.

insulation When an animal or bird has a layer of fur or feathers to prevent the loss of body heat.

migration When a living thing makes a seasonal journey to a new habitat.

nocturnal To be active mainly at night.

pesticides Substances that can be used to kill fungi, bacteria, or insects.

plumage The pattern and colors created by the feathers on a bird.

pollinate When pollen is transferred from the male to the female parts of the flower.

predators Living things that regularly prey on others for food.

preening When a bird cleans or tidies its feathers with its bill, to keep them in good order.

RAMSAR An international agreement concerned with the protection of wetland areas.

respiration system The heart, lungs, and blood vessels that work together to keep the blood oxygenated.

roost When birds perch to go to sleep.

species A group of organisms, such as insects, plants, animals, or birds, that closely resemble one another.

wetland An area of land that remains waterlogged for most of the year.

wind resistance The "pull" that slows a bird down when it tries to move quickly through the air.

FURTHER INFORMATION

BOOKS TO READ

Chinery, Michael. *Secrets of the Rainforest.* New York: Cherrytree, 2001.

Deiters, Jim and Erika. *MacAws (Animals of the Rain Forests).* New York: Raintree Steck-Vaughn, 2002.

Dollar, Sam. *Toucans (Animals of the Rain Forests).* New York: Raintree Steck-Vaughn Publishers, 2001.

Frost, Helen. *Parrots (Rain Forest Animals).* Dover, NH: Pebble Books, 2002.

Kalman, Bobbie. *Rainforest Birds (Birds Up Close).* New York: Crabtree Publishing, 1998.

Kite, Lorien. *A Rain Forest Tree.* New York: Crabtree Publishing, 1999.

Knight, Tim. *Journey into the Rain Forest.* New York: Oxford University Press, 2001.

VIDEO

Forest Family Forever, Environmental Media Corp., 2001.

ADDRESSES OF ORGANIZATIONS

Rainforest Action Network
221 Pine Street, Suite 500
San Francisco, CA 94104
(415) 398-4404

Rainforest Alliance
65 Bleecker Street
New York, NY 10012
(212) 677-1900

The Songbird Foundation
2367 Eastlake Avenue East
Seattle, WA 98102
(206) 374-3674

INDEX